ANDREAS LITRAS is a graduate of the John Bolton Theatre School (1992). Since graduating, he has worked as an actor with various theatre companies including Woolly Jumpers (Victoria), Melbourne Workers' Theatre (Victoria), Theatre at Large (New Zealand), Salamanca Theatre Company (Tasmania), Zootango Theatre Company (Tasmania), Terrapin Puppet Company (Tasmania) and Theatre Alfresco (Tasmania). He has worked as both teacher and director and has several writing credits to his name including the co-adaption of the Roald Dahl children's classic *The BFG* for Terrapin Puppet Company. Together with Brianne Cuthbert, he co-founded Anthos Theatre in 1998.

For nearly forty years JOHN BOLTON has been acting, teaching and directing throughout the world. He directed Artworks and Theatre Workshop Edinburgh, and acted with Welfare State in England. In 1991 he founded his own school in Melbourne, and was Head of Acting at the Victorian College of the Arts. He has received numerous awards for direction including two Green Room awards for Best Direction and Best Production. He has been Director of Movement for STC and the MTC and was awarded the 2002 Kenneth Myer Medallion for Services to Theatre in Victoria. He is the recipient of the Australian Arts Council Fellowship for 2011/12.

Andreas Litras in the 1998 Melbourne International Festival production at the George Fairfax Studio, Victorian Arts Centre, Melbourne. (Photo Ilana Rose)

ODYSSEY

ANDREAS LITRAS &
JOHN BOLTON

Currency Press • Sydney

CURRENCY PLAYS

First published in 2012
by Currency Press Pty Ltd,
PO Box 2287, Strawberry Hills, NSW, 2012, Australia
enquiries@currency.com.au
www.currency.com.au

NATIONAL LIBRARY OF AUSTRALIA CIP DATA

Author: Litras, Andreas.
Title: Odyssey / Andreas Litras and John Bolton.
ISBN: 9780868199511 (pbk.)
Other Authors/Contributors:
                  Bolton, John.
Dewey Number: A822.4

Typeset by Dean Nottle for Currency Press.

Odyssey was created with assistance from
the Commonwealth Government through the
Australia Council, its arts funding and advisory
body, and also from the Tasmanian Minister for
State Development through Arts Tasmania.

Australian Government

Australia Council
for the Arts

Tasmania
Explore the possibilities

Contents

The publisher has made every reasonable effort to contact copyright holders for permission to reproduce the song lyrics contained in this book. Any enquiries should be directed to Currency Press.

Cover design by Emma Vine for Currency Press.

Cover images: Andreas Litras in the 1998 Melbourne International Festival production at the George Fairfax Studio, Victorian Arts Centre, Melbourne. (Photos: Ilana Rose).

Currency Press acknowledges the Traditional Owners of the Country on which we live and work. We pay our respects to all Aboriginal and Torres Strait Islander Elders, past and present.

Andreas Litras in the 1998 Melbourne International Festival production at the George Fairfax Studio, Victorian Arts Centre, Melbourne. (Photo Ilana Rose)

INTRODUCTION

First performed in 1998, Andreas Litras and John Bolton's one-man play, *Odyssey*, continues to engage, entertain and educate audiences. The tour continues. *Odyssey* has become an odyssey in itself.

While the script cannot convey the physicality and sheer energy of Litras' live performance, it unveils the unique structure of the play, and its multilayered meanings, folk references and earthy language.

Odyssey interweaves three narratives. Homer's *Odyssey*, the ancient tale, provides the template for an enactment of Litras' parents', Angelo and Paraskevi's, migration to Australia, and the performer's personal search for a sense of identity and belonging as the son of Greek immigrants who settle in regional Victoria.

At the heart of Homer's *Odyssey* is that infernal ache known as nostalgia. The ancient narrative is driven by Odysseus' ten-year journey back home after he has spent ten years fighting the Trojan wars. In all he is away for twenty years, enough time for a new generation to grow into adulthood. He is beset by unexpected detours, sojourns with beautiful women, and the whims of the gods. Yet his longing to return to his beloved Ithaca remains strong.

The word 'nostalgia' is derived from the Greek *'nostos'*, the return, and *'algos'*, meaning pain. Nostalgia literally means 'the pain of longing for the return'. It can be a pain so intense that not so long ago the condition was regarded by some physicians as an illness.

In our era of instant global communication, nostalgia is often misunderstood or dismissed as mere sentimentality, especially by those who have not been forced to leave their homelands. It is hard to comprehend the depth of this longing unless we fully step into the shoes of someone who has made the journey. Litras' enactments of his parents' travails allow the audience to empathise with the daunting challenge faced by countless immigrants.

Angelo and Paraskevi were born in villages located on the mainland coast of Greece, opposite the island of Lefkada, which, coincidentally, is situated not so far from the present-day island of Ithaca. Angelo was one of the many thousands of Greeks who made their way to distant

Afstralia in the post-war years. He left in the wake of a devastating civil war in which brother turned on brother, and entire communities were torn apart. The civil war and the pain it inflicted on Greece was compounded by extreme poverty.

Like Odysseus, and like so many contemporary emigrants, Angelo left his homeland with the hope of one day returning. He initially saw himself as a sojourner. His goal was to make enough money to lift his family out of poverty. As he leaves, he says to one of his fellow villagers, 'Goodbye Georgie, look after the sheep till I return'. He tells his mother, 'Don't cry. I'll be back with these suitcases full of money.'

The new country is seen as a foreign land, or *xenitia*, literally a land 'outside' Greece. *Xenitia* implies far more—an intense longing with a sense of absence and loss. Drawing upon the extensive repertoire of Greek songs of exile and journeying, Litras sings: 'I left as a young man/ And I live with one hope/ My mother to see again/ And my sweet homeland.'

Equally daunting, and often overlooked, was the fate of the women who emigrated. Like a good number of Greek women, Paraskevi left to marry a man she knew only from a photo. In this respect, the play departs from the Homeric template. Paraskevi is no Penelope, waiting at home while her husband is off on his adventures. She too is a voyager, and she becomes an equal participant in the venture, keeping house, bearing and rearing four children while helping out in the family fish'n'chip shop. When tragedy strikes the family, she becomes the key to their survival.

Finally, there is Andreas Litras' own journey of self-discovery. He enacts the journey in reverse and returns to his parents' home village. He seeks to come to terms with his former self, the boy who once was ashamed of his Greek origins, who 'didn't want to be a wog' in the schoolyard.

Litras is of the 'second generation', caught between the past world of his parents, and the lure of the new world into which he was born. He undertakes the journey to make sense of it all, and returns with a deeper understanding of that elusive concept, 'home'. *Odyssey* reveals how subtle and rewarding such a journey of discovery can be.

Litras and Bolton draw upon many sources and theatrical skills to convey their multi-faceted story. The play is a hybrid of slapstick, pantomime, pure storytelling, personal reflection, folk motifs and the creation of multiple personas. Litras takes on the guise of an irreverent stagehand to spin the ancient narrative. In turn, the stagehand takes his cue from the traditional shadow-puppet theatre character, Karagiozi, a cunning prankster who is well positioned to convey the guile of the wily and resourceful Odysseus, a 'man of many ways' and 'many tricks'.

This hybrid of theatrical forms and folk references provides a model for the increasing number of Australians who wish to explore the journeys of their immigrant families. The play presents a specific narrative with universal resonances. *Odyssey* is as relevant today as in the post-war years when Angelo and Paraskevi became modern day versions of ancient Odysseus.

Currently there are millions of displaced peoples worldwide. Many languish for years in refugee camps. Others are on the move, desperately trying to find a country where they can feel secure, and where their families can flourish.

As the latest version of 'boat people' make their way to our shores from the Middle East and Asian countries, Litras' performance takes on renewed relevance and urgency. These latest arrivals have been labelled as queue jumpers and worse. Political leaders who should know better, have played upon xenophobia, literally, 'fear of the outsider', rather than encourage understanding. Only when we hear the individual story, as we do in *Odyssey*, do we comprehend the ongoing universal drama of migration.

Odyssey encourages such understanding through that most ancient of art forms—live storytelling. It invites personal responses from audience members, and encourages people to share their own stories. When I saw the play performed, during its first season back in 1998, it immediately resonated with the journey of my own parents, whose families had been murdered during the dark years of the Holocaust.

I also identified with Litras' perspective as a child of immigrants. Back in 1986 I too was compelled to journey back to the villages in Eastern Poland where my ancestors had lived for centuries. I returned with a conviction that it is an Australian journey, one that makes us alive to the courageous odysseys of our own forebears.

Indeed, migration ranks with the extraordinary history of Indigenous people as one of Australia's two grand narratives. It is little known that the largest number of people who forsook their homeland in modern times were the fifteen million who, towards the latter half of the nineteenth century, left the British Isles—Ireland, Scotland, England and Wales—due to the draconian land clearances, political persecution, and the massive socio-economic dislocation caused by the industrial revolution.

In Ireland, the 'Great Famine' and mass starvation between 1845 and 1852, caused the death of one million out of a population of eight million, while one and a half million took to boats. Some fetched up on the shores of Australia, lured by the promise of better lives. In all, over three million people left Ireland between 1845 and 1870.

Odyssey also touches upon the more positive aspects of the immigrant experience. Many come to love the new land, or are at least reconciled to their fate, not only because of the economic opportunities it provides, but also because of the scope for personal freedom.

At one point Litras says:

> I asked my mother why she never went back to Greece to live. She told me that she had spent more years of her life living in Australia than she ever had in Greece, and that as a woman she was freer living here than she ever would have been in Greece. But also she said that all her children were born here and that her husband was buried here in this soil, and that makes this our home.

As Lindsay Clarke, writing in *The Press*, Christchurch, puts it:

> ... these are rich tales, appealing for their simple humanity and humour as much as their finely judged theatrical impact. What is truly remarkable about this performance is its seemingly artless balancing of epic scale and trivial actions within one dramatic frame.

Reviewing the play in the *NZ Listener*, Faith Oxenbridge concludes:

> Litras spun the three narratives together to make gold. With the help of a few boxes, a suitcase of props, and director John Bolton, he filled the unadorned stage with a swag of colourful and engaging characters. The production was as philosophical as it was physical, and sifted gently yet surely through the steps of pain and hope we all take in finding our way home.

The publication of the text will add another dimension to the pleasure and understanding that *Odyssey* continues to provide as it continues its long journey.

Arnold Zable
February 2012

Arnold Zable is an acclaimed novelist, storyteller and human rights activist who has written extensively on the immigrant experience, and the fate of contemporary asylum seekers.

Andreas Litras in the 1998 Peacock Theatre production in Hobart.
(Photo Simon Cuthbert)

DIRECTOR'S NOTE

Homer's *Odyssey* is less about adventure than homesickness. It is exciting, frightening and awe-inspiring, but it is about the journey home, not exploring new lands in search of knowledge and power; a return to the place already known, however deeply forgotten or buried.

R. D. Laing, the Scottish psychiatrist, once asked his ten-year-old son what he thought his father did. He replied, 'You help people find their way home'. And so it is with all of us. Like Odysseus we get distracted, lured offcourse, and sometimes are so frightened of the next step towards home that we wait until the pain of separation is too strong to deny before we drag our feet a step closer. We have to use guile to defeat our monsters, as Odysseus did, and naturally we offend the gods with our pride and clinging to old habits until they punish us with more tasks to perform, more conscious steps to take.

Odysseus' twenty-year return sounds a long time until we compare it to our lifetimes' work of getting closer to home, only to find the essential resting place has shifted and we set off again. Step by step.

The modern story of immigration would appear superficially to be something different—not a returning, but a journey to a new land, a new hope. In a physical sense this is true. But on a deeper level, the modern immigrant undertakes a personal odyssey of finding home on a foreign shore. This new home is not concerned with sentimental representations of the old homeland, but with the acceptance of new ways (without which we get stuck in a time warp) in tandem with the retention of elements of the original culture (without which we are grasses in the wind).

This play deals with these two complementary odysseys as well as a third: Andreas' personal journey of discovering his general, family and personal histories. His odyssey has been the creation of this play, and it has been a pleasure and a privilege to have been a part of it.

John Bolton

For my mother, Paraskevi, an ordinary woman who has led an epic and extraordinary life.

Andreas

Odyssey was first produced at the Peacock Theatre, Hobart, Tasmania, on 25 March 1998 with the following participants:

Performer, Andreas Litras
Director, John Bolton
Set and Costume Design, Constantine Koukias
Lighting Design, Jan Wawrzynczak
Stage Manager, Tim Munro
Set Construction, Jon Bowling
Photography, Simon Cuthbert
Producer, Brianne Cuthbert

Odyssey was created by Andreas Litras and John Bolton with assistance from the Commonwealth Government through the Australia Council, its arts funding and advisory body, and also from the Tasmanian Minister for State Development through Arts Tasmania.

A READER'S GUIDE

Homer's Odyssey

'Odyssey', according to *Webster's Dictionary*, means 'a series of adventurous journeys usually marked by many changes of fortune'. The Greek word *'Odusseia'* [Οδύσσεια] simply means 'the story of Odysseus', hero of the Trojan War, who took ten years to find his way back home to Ithaca. Homer's epic poem *Odyssey* consists of over 12,109 lines of hexameter verse and is believed to have been written in the 8th or early 7th century BC, making the poem over 2,700 years old. It is believed that the story itself existed in oral form for many years before being scribed by Homer. As the story was passed from storyteller to storyteller, each bard would add their own embellishments and details to suit their audience.

The Songs

The songs used in the play are *Λαϊκά* [Laika] or folk songs, many of which deal with life in the *Ξενιτία* [Ξenitya]. The closest translation in English is 'the foreign lands', meaning simply any place outside Greece and away from home. The word also carries with it notions of longing, absence and loss—hallmarks of the migrant experience.

About Karagiozi ((Karagiozis)

Karagiozi [*Καραγκιόζη*] is a central character from the 19th-century shadow puppet theatre, *theatro skion* [Θέατρο σκιών]—literally the theatre of shadows—which was popular throughout the Asia Minor region. Karagiozi's name is Turkish for 'black eyes' and describes the distinctive dark circles under Karagiozi's eyes.

Karagiozi is a character in the tradition of Mr Punch from England's Punch and Judy show. Ugly, hunchbacked and with one abnormally long arm, Karagiozi doles out punishment at will. He is a gambler, a liar and lazy, but he is also cunning and has a wit that can run circles around others. He is famous for his pranks, which he sets up to tease those around him.

Traditionally the themes of each Karagiozi play were adapted to various current social and political issues, as well as to historical events of Ottoman-ruled Greece. These historical Karagiozi plays were very popular during times of crisis, as they lifted the audience's spirits and offered hope, making the figure of Karagiozi an important cultural icon for the Greek people during the Ottoman occupation of Greece. Through Karagiozi, a puppeteer would satirise authority figures and situations. Karagiozi represented the common folk in a collision with everyone and everything unjust, whether social or political.

Note on the Text

This play is bi-lingual. The actor performs in both Greek and English. The Greek text included in the script is spoken. However, the phonetic transliteration and English translation in parentheses, which follow the Greek, are not spoken, but have been included to assist readers unfamiliar with the Greek language.

Andreas Litras & John Bolton

CHARACTERS

KARAGIOZI, a notorious prankster

O'DYSSEA, ruler of Ithaca

PENELOPE, his wife

ANGELO, Andreas' father

PARASKEVI, Andreas' mother

PARASKEVI'S MOTHER

AGELKOULA, Paraskevi's sister

CYCLOPS, a one-eyed monster

CIRCE, a beautiful island goddess

TIRESIAS, a blind seer

O'DYSSEA'S MOTHER

AGAMEMNON, a Greek king

TROJANS, MEN, SAILORS, A BAR FLY

All characters are played by the one actor.

On some occasions character names are used in the playtext; on other occasions Andreas Litras speaks directly to the audience as himself.

SCENE ONE: KARAGIOZI

There are three large boxes on the stage in the shape of a 'V' with the point of the 'V' upstage centre. There is a smell of incense in the air and a haze created by the incense.

KARAGIOZI *enters, holding a bucket of water, a large broom and wearing a beanie. He sees the audience.*

KARAGIOZI: Ohh. Hhh, hello ev'rybody.

He speaks to the lighting operator.

Βρέ [Hey you], Timothy, put the lights on, I carn see.

The house lights come on.

Hello, welcome to tonight… to the theata… the festival… Look, we got a problem here. Because, to tell the truth, you not s'posed to be here. 'Ere, I mean of course you s'posed to be 'ere, but not yet. You too early. Andreas is not ready to start the show, bloody stupik out the fron' let you into the theata too soon. Look, I'm sorry, ev'rybody, but you goin' to have to wait now for Andreas, we got nuthin' set up, an' his a professional you know, ohh yeah, his a professional ackta. I mean, you carn ask a professional to start the theata early jus' because stupik out the fron' carn tell the time, come on. So now you goin' to 'ave to wait, for Andreas. Look, nothing set up. Is not even clean. Ahhh, you carn get good help today!

He starts to sweep the stage, then turns to an audience member.

'Scuse me, mate, you got the time? Than' you veri mutch, is time to set up.

He starts to unpack the box sitting downstage on the left hand side.

You can talk to yourselves. Awright?

He continues to unpack.

You see this?

He points to the box he is unpacking—this is the prop box.

You like this? I make this, for Andreas, you know for the theata. You see, one day Andreas say to me, 'Ah, ρέ Καραγκιόζη

[*Karagiozi*]'—that's my name Karagiozi—anyhow, he says to me, 'I need something to put all my prop'. You know prop? 'Prop'— είναι τα πράγματα που θέλει ένας ηθοποιός για το θέατρο [*inay ta pragmata pou theli enas ithopios ya to theatro*—the things an actor needs to make theatre]—you know the ackta, usin' the prop for the theata. Anyhow he says, 'I need something for my prop,' and I say to him, 'Don' worry, Andreas, you need somethin' for your prop, I make you number one prop box'. This is prop box. This is where all the props from the theata is goin'. Looki here, you got prop, prop, prop, prop, prop. I tell you somethin'? A secret, from the theata. You can tell how good an ackta is from how many props his use, is true! 'Cause only a professional use a lot of prop. Look, I show you. [*He holds up a prop.*] This is a prop. [*He holds up another.*] A prop. [*Then another.*] Yes, it's a prop! You see how many his got? I tell you, you in for a good time tonight.

> By this point KARAGIOZI *has set up a table and chair downstage. On the table sits a small black box, a washbasin, a mug, a soap holder and a washcloth. On the floor there are three suitcases.*

All the props for the theata. Ahhh, the theata. You know the Greeks invent the theata. No, is true. The Greeks, we are very clever people, we invent a lot of things; we invent democracy, theata, the triangle. [*He makes a triangle with his fingers.*] The Greeks, we very clever people—I mean looka dat? [*Pointing to the prop box*] Yeah, the Greeks, the first for the theata. I suppose you like it, uh? I mean the theata—you like it—well of course you like it, tha's why you here. I don' like theata so much. No, for me I prefer television, his much betta. I mean if you watchin' television an' you don' like what you watchin'—tsak—you change the channel, but theata.

I mean, I tell you somethin'.

> He points to someone who is sitting in the middle of the theatre.

I'm sorri to pick on you but you got a terrible seat. You, yes you, you talkin' to me, I'm talkin' to you. You probli got the worst seat in the whol' bloody theata. If I'm like you I'm goin' out to ask for my money back. You see where you sittin'? You sittin' right in the middle from everyone—if you don't like this show you got to get pass all those people to get out of the theata.

He points to someone near an exit.

You see this person here—his very clever—you see where his sittin'? His sittin' right at the end of the row next to the door—if he don' like this show—[*clicking his fingers*]—his out the door! This bloke his a numba one professional theata-watcha. [*To the person in the middle*] You can learn a lot from this one. Very clever. [*To the person at the end of the row*] You mus' be Greek. You not Greek, you sure? You go ask your motha.

Yes, the Greeks the first for the theata. That's why one day Andreas says to me, 'I really want to tell a story in the theata'. I say to him, 'Awright, you go ahead, jus' don' botha me'. He says, 'No, Karagiozi, you don' understand. I want to tell a Greek story.' I say to him, 'A Greek story! Μπράβο λεβέντη [*Bravo levendi*—Good on you lad]. Now you talking. But which Greek story you going to tell?' You know there are so many good Greek stories, it's hard to choose. I say to him, 'You soud tell the story from Oedipus'. You know Oedipus, his the bloke who kill his father, then sleep with his mother, an' when he find out, he take two knitting needles, he poke out his eyes and his blind for the rest of his life. Now that's a lovely Greek story.

He says, 'No, I don' want to tell that story, I want to tell the story of my motha and fatha when they come from Greece to Afstralia'. I say, 'Uh, come on, Andreas, that's not a propa Greek story. You got to tell a propa Greek story for the theata, one of the old ones, one of the good ones, not something 'bout your motha and fatha!' But he doesn' want to listen 'cause he's the ackta. I mean, what you can do?

He begins to pour water from the bucket into the washbasin.

Oh, I hope this sound don' make no-one want to go to the toilet. You know some people they hear this and—tsak—straight away they have to go. Everyone awrite, you sure? Good bladdas.

Anyhow, I say to Andreas, 'You carn tell the story about you motha an' fatha—you got to tell them something beautiful like… O'dyssea'. I love that story. You know O'dyssea. O'dyssea? [*He crosses himself.*] O'dyssea! Some people call him—Ulysses, but that's not the propa Greek name, that's the bloody Roman name.

Stupik Romans carn think of nothin' for themselves so they pinch everything from the Greeks and just change the name. His propa Greek name is O'dyssea. O-dyssea. You know his the bloke who go to Troy, Τροία [*Treeah*] we call it in Greek. An' he fight the war of Troy to get a Helen back. You know Helen? She's a bewdiful lady. She was so bewdiful the Trojans kidnap her and the Greeks send one thousand ships to get her back. And they fight for ten years— you can believe that? to fight one war for ten years. Then after Troy he try to get back to Ithaca, but he have a lot of trouble. You know he meet the Κύκλωπας [*Kyklopas*], you know, μα πώς τον λένε [*ma pos ton lene*—what do they call him], with the one big eye…

He pauses for an audience member to respond 'the Cyclops'.

The Cyclops! Yeah, that's it. Anyway O'dyssea pokes the eye out from the Cyclops because the Cyclops eat his make [*mate*]. I mean fair enough, is'na? You eat my make, I am going to poke out your eye too, that's the least I can do for you. I mean, if you say to me, 'I'm sorry Karagiozi, I eat your friend', whaddam I goin' to say? 'Oh, doesn' madda, I godda nother one'. No way. I poke out your eye.

But you know who I love the most in that story? I love Penelope, the wife from O'dyssea—she's the one she does the wavin'. [*He starts waving his right hand from side to side.*] Yeah, you know she's waitin' for her husband to come home so she's wavin' to pass the time, just wavin' and wavin'.

He looks at the audience and realises that they do not understand.

You know, wavin'. What you call it in Englis'? When you make the carpet an' the mats. What you call it?

An audience member yells out 'weaving'.

Yeah, that's what I said—wavin'. Anyhow she's wavin' and waitin' for her husband to come home and all these blokes thay wan' to marry her 'cause they thin' O'dyssea his dead. But Penelope she is a very cleva woman—she says, 'Awright, boys, I goin' to choose one of you boys to be my new husban' when I finish my wavin'. So she's wavin', wavin', wavin', during the day, but at night… [*miming undoing a thread*] undo, undo, undo. Wavin, wavin', wavin' during the day, at night—undo, undo, undo. Wavin', wavin', wavin'… undo, undo, undo. It takes three years for those stupik blokes to figure out why she's not finis' that wavin'! But when they find out, they angry. 'Listen, Penelope, no more wavin', you have to pick one from us to marry you. Your husban' his dead.'

But his no dead—that the best part—his still tryin' to come home, but his got the undaworld and you got Scylla and Charibdis… I mean you must know the story. Hey, what's the time? Well, we got a coupla minutes before Andreas start, I have to tell you the story, I mean—*The Odyssey*!

SCENE TWO: KARAGIOZI'S ODYSSEY

KARAGIOZI: Η Οδύσσεια του Ομήρου [*Ee ohthisia tou Omero*]. The Odyssey of Homer.

Πες μου Θεά για τον άνθρωπο τον πολύτροπο Οδυσσέα [*Pes mou theya ya ton unthropo ton polytropo O'dyssea*]. Sing to me, muse of the man of twists and turns, O'dyssea.

One day, O'dyssea is at home when suddenly: brr brr,

He pulls a toy telephone from his pocket.

'Hello, O'dyssea speaking. Oh, Capitan Agamemnon. Έλα, άντε μωρέ μη μου το λες. Βρε το τομάρι [*Elah, ardeh morreh min moh toh les. Vre toh tomari*—Tell me, oh don't tell me. Oh the scoundrel]. Yeah, don' worry, I fix it for you, yeah, we can get her back, awright relax, I see you at, ah… [*looking at a pretend wristwatch*] … Troy.'

He hangs up.

Penelope, I'm sorry, darlin'. I got to go to Troy.

He kisses his wife goodbye.

[*To the audience*] Well, don' watch.

He turns his back to the audience and mimes kissing his wife. She pinches his bum.

Penelope! Oh, Telemachus, my baby boy.

He mimes holding a baby and sings.

[*Sung*]
 Νάνι-νάνι το μωρό και θα πάει στο σχολειό!
 [*Nani nani to moro kyeh tha payi sto skholio*—Go to sleep, my little boy, and you'll go to school!]

Αχ το παιδεί μου το μικρό, ε—
[*Ah to pehthi mou to mikro*—Oh, my little child]

The baby bites his finger.

—ας το δάχτυλο μωρέ [*Us to thaktilo*—Ow, let go of my finger]!
Let go!

[*To* PENELOPE] μα πάρ' το παιδί [*Par to ped hi*] Take the boy, I
got to go to Troy!

O'dyssea, climb aboard the boat, they have big φουρτούνα
[*fortouna*—a big storm].

He drags two of the boxes downstage and forms a wall.

[*As* ODYSSEUS] 'Wooah, βοήθεια [*voyetheeah*—help]! Aahh, hol'
on, boys. Oh, where are we, boys? Ah look, the wall from Troy—
tha's quick, we there already. Alright, boys, leave this up to me. I
fix it.

He knocks.

Hello, ah, it's O'dyssea here, I come to get a Helen back for the
Greeks.

He waits a moment then knocks again.

Hello. O'dyssea, come to get a Helen for the... Bloody rude! Suddenly
the door to Troy open.

He moves the boxes, opening the gates Troy.

All the Trojans come out to fight with the Greeks.

*He mimes a slapstick battle scene—arrows being fired, blood
spurting, heads being cut off.*

Yah, chuck, chuck, wop wop, pow, erghgh.

The doors close.

The doors to Troy close. Ohhh, so many Greeks dead on the ground.
Ah, αχ τα παλικάρια μας [*ach ta palikaria mas*—oh, our brave
lads]. Oh, so many Greeks are dead—the Trojans are dead too but
who cares about them? Ohhh, the Greeks are dead. Whoa, hoa, hoa.
And then the next day...

The doors open.

... ahhh, chuck chuck...

The doors close.

… whoa, hoa hoa…

The doors open.

… ahhh, chuck, chuck chuck…

The doors close.

… whoa, whoa whoa whoa… You know the same go on for ten bloody years! After ten years the Greeks say, 'Oh, bugga Helen, I'm going home'.

O'dyssea says, 'We carn go home, we carn let the Trojans beat us, we are Greek, remember? Just give me one minute. I know I can thin' of something. Just give me one… I mean the Trojans… we carn let the Trojans…

His voice starts to change, imitating the neighing of a horse.

'… wait a minute, yeeesss, I got a good ideaaahhhh. Hey, boys, go back to the boat and make it look like you're going back to Greece an' when I give you the signal, you come back and we get Troy.'

He opens a suitcase and pulls out a toilet brush, which he puts between his legs so the brush sticks out behind him, and a broom which he holds so that the bristles stick out above his head—he is the Trojan Horse.

You geddit? Shhh.

He knocks on the wall.

TROJAN 1: Hello, who's there?
O'DYSSEA: Neeighhhhhh.
TROJAN 1: Oh, it looks like all the Greeks gone home and they leave us a lovely present. Is'na nice? Less take it inside.
TROJAN 2: I don' thin' we sould, someone tol' me you sould be very careful of a Greek bearing a gift.
TROJAN 1: Oh, come on, it's justa horse.
O'DYSSEA: [*to the audience*] Ahh, the stupik Trojans. You know you don' ever have to worry about a Greek bearing a gift. But be very careful about a gift bearing a Greek.

The wall closes. We hear the voices behind the wall.

TROJAN 1: Ohh, is'na lovely horse?

O'DYSSEA: I'm not a horse, you stupik, I'm O'dyssea!

> KARAGIOZI *throws the wall to the ground and stands on it.*

KARAGIOZI: And O'dyssea tear down the walls of Troy and the Greeks are the winnahs. Is'na fantastic start to the story? [*To an audience member*] Hey, what's the time, make? Why you not tell me? Andreas waiting to start the show.

> *He resets the stage.*

You know, to tell the truth, that part of the story, you know the wooden horse and the Trojan War, is not really from *The Odyssey.* That part is come from the *The Illiad.* You know *The Illiad* is the story that comes before *The Odyssey*—i before e, that sort of thin'.

> *He checks to make sure that everything is as it should be.*

I think it's time to start the show.

SCENE THREE: ANGELO'S STORY

KARAGIOZI *crosses to the table and opens a small black box. It is a gramophone. As he speaks he begins to wind up the gramophone.*

KARAGIOZI: In Greece, after the second World War, the Greek people they have another war— ο εμφύλιος [*o emfilios*]. Greek against Greek, brother against brother—civil war. It was terrible. Andreas' father Angelo—that was his name, Angelo—he was a fighter, a fighter in the civil war, an' Andreas' grandfather, that's Angelo's father, he was shot… [*clapping his hands imitating a gunshot*] … killed by the communists. Oh, it's true, why in the villatz today, back in Greece, you can still see the tree in the schoolyard where his grandfather was shot, where they excecuted him. That tree has still got the same bullet hole in it today.

After this war Greece was shockin', no jobs, no food, nothin'. The mothers used to put the pot on the stove you know to cook dinnah and the kids they say, 'Mum, we hungry, when we goin' to eat?' The mother says, 'I have to cook and then you can eat'. After a while, 'Mum, we hungry, when we goin' to eat?' The motha says, 'Look, if we don' cook the food proply you goin' to get a stomach ache— you just have to wait'. [*Pause.*] 'Mum, we really hungry, now when are we goin to eat?' 'Look, you just have to wait!' And finally the kids are so tired they fall asleep and the mother takes the pot off the stove and tips out the water inside.

After a couple of years Angelo, Andreas' father, he says, 'Aw listen, I had it enough of this, I'm goin' to go to, to, to Afstralia'. 'Oh, where is Afstralia, Angelo?' 'I don't know but, I'm goin''. When the time comes for Angelo to leave they have one big party.

The gramophone begins playing.

When the day come for Angelo to leave they carry the gramophone down to the docks and the whole the villatz Κανδήλα [*Kundila*] [1], they come out to say goodbye. Everyone there, walking behind the gramophone in a procession, people there, laughin', singin', cryin' of course. Everyone want to say 'bye-'bye, Angelo. Καλό ταξίδι [*Kalo taxithi*—Bon voyage].

He takes off the beanie.

He turns picks up the suitcase and becomes ANGELO *walking down to the ship to bid farewell.*

SCENE FOUR: ANGELO COMES TO AUSTRALIA

ANGELO: Γεια σου Γιώργο, κοίτα τα πρόβατα βρε μέχρι να γυρίσω [*Yia sou yiorgo, kita ta provata vre mechri na yirisou*—Goodbye Georgie, look after the sheep, lad, till I return].

He steps aboard the boat and waves goodbye.

Γεια σας όλοι σας, θα γυρίσω με μια βαλίτσα γεμάτη χρήματα [*Yia sas olli sas, tha yrisou me mia valitsa yemati hrimata*—Goodbye, all of you, I will return with a suitcase full of money].

He sees his mother.

Αχ μανα μη μου κλαίς. Θα γυρίσω με μια βαλίτσα μεμάτη χρήματα. [*Ah mana mi mou kles. Tha yrisou me mia valitsa yemati hrimata. Na me perimenete*—Oh Mother, don't cry. I will return with a suitcase full of money. Wait for me].

He remains staring at the shore as the boat pulls away.

---

[1] A village on the west coast of the mainland of Greece, near Lefkada.

Αχ μάνα που στο διάολο πηγαίνω; [*Ah mana pou sto theaolo paow*— Oh Mother, where the devil am I going?]

He sits on his suitcase, takes out a letter and reads it.

The gramophone finishes playing its song.

ANGELO *folds the letter in the shape of a boat and sails to Australia while singing.*

SONG: 'Κατω απ το γέρο πλάτανο' ('Under the Ancient Plane Tree')

> Κατω απ το γέρο πλάτανο
> Έγειρα να πλαγιάσω
> Να λησμονεί
> Σα 'ναν καημός
> Και να ξαποστάσω

> [Under the ancient plane tree
> I went to lay down
> To forget my sorrows
> And to recover]

> Όταν κοιμάται ο άνθρωπος
> Και όταν τα μάτια κλείνει
> Απότομα και απ' την καρδία
> Κάθε μαράζι σβήνει.

> [When a man sleeps
> And when he closes his eyes
> Suddenly and from the heart
> Every eating sorrow is extinguished.]

As the boat reaches the shore the song finishes.

Αυστραλία [*Afstralyia*]!

He stands.

Afstralia! Po po po!

He moves to a low doorway and stoops to enter. He looks around and then sets his suitcase down in a bedroom.

Καλώς ήρθατε [*Kalos irtharte*—Welcome].

He opens the suitcase, removes a packet of dirt and a pot, and plants a seed. He sings gently.

SONG: 'Μια χούφτα χώμα ελληνικό' ('A Handful of Greek Earth')

Μια χούφτα χώμα ελληνικό
Για φυλαχτό θα πάρω
Τώρα που πάω στην Ξενιτιά
Να μη φοβάμαι κανένα Χάρο

[A handful of Greek earth
As a keepsake I'll take
Now that I'm going to the foreign lands
So that I will fear no ill fate]

Δεν θα ξεχάσω το χωριό
Όσο καιρό θα αργήσω
Στο σπίτι μου το πατρικό
Γρήγορα θα γυρίσω.

[I will not forget my village
No matter how long I am gone
To my father's house
I'll quickly return.]

He steps forward, out of the bedroom, and mimes pouring tea for a queue of people. At first he is unable to speak. He smiles and offers tea, then moves to the next person.

Cuppa?

As he moves along the queue his language skills develop.

G'day, make, you wanna a cuppa?

ANDREAS: When my father first arrived he worked on the railways making the tea.

ANGELO: Hey, boys, the billy boy's here, time for cuppa.

He sings a popular hit song of the time as he works.

Hey, Harry you bludga, we never finis' the railway with you, make. Here, have a cuppa, maybe make you work faster.

He resumes singing as he moves centre stage and mimes wrapping fish and chips.

Yes please. Now two pices fis', chips, an' two, three potato cakes, here you go, make, no, no the potata cakes a little bit small today, I put a cupla extra.

He sits and plays cards.

Αχ παιδιά απόψε θ' ανοίξει η τύχη μου. Α μωρέ σ' έπιασα [*Ach pethia tovrathi tha anixi i tichi mou. Ah moree se piasa*—Ah, lads, tonight my luck will change. Ah, got ya].

He stands and wraps fish and chips.

Yes please. You ready to order, make? Yep, you want vinegah, no problem. Salt an' vinegah. Alright, one hambergah with the lot coming up!

He sits again and plays more cards.

Αχ παιδιά απόψε θ' ανοίξει η τύχη μου. Α μωρέ σ' έπιασα [*Ach pethia tovrathi tha anixi i tichi mou. Ah moree se piasa*—Ah, lads, tonight my luck will change. Ah, got ya].

He dances.

Ω, Όπα. [*Opa—a celebratory sound.*]

SONG: 'Στα Ξένα μερ' ('To the Foreign Lands')

> Στα ξένα μέρη
> Έφυγα μικρός
> Και ζω με μια ελπίδα
> Τη μάνα μου, να ξανά δω
> Και τη γλυκιά πατρίδα.
>
> [To the foreign lands
> I left as a young man
> And I live with one hope
> My mother to see again
> And my sweet homeland.]

The dance turns into a drunken stagger and then suddenly ANGELO *is back wrapping fish and chips.*

Yes please, make. Oh yeah, not bad, you know, yeah, awright, I see you tomorrow.

ANGELO mimes turning off the gas cooker.

He walks to the front of the stage and transforms into ANDREAS.

SCENE FIVE: TWO PHOTOGRAPHS

ANDREAS: One night after closing up the shop my father went to visit his cousin Dino. With him he took two photographs. He showed both the photos to Dino and said, 'Which one should I pick?' And Dino looked at the two photographs in Angelo's hands and after a while he said, 'This one, yeah take this one, she looks nicer'. She is my mother, Paraskevi.

When Paraskevi saw the photograph of Angelo for the first time she saw a man balding, bow-legged, and twenty years older than herself. She took the photograph to her sister Maria and said, 'I can't marry this man'. Maria took one look and said, 'Μα πρέπει να τον πάρεις' [Ma prepey na ton pareis]—'You have to marry him'. My mother was one of six daughters and the fewer girls that stayed in Greece the more dowry there would be for all the girls who stayed behind. So the sisters who stayed in Greece would get more land, more livestock, more money... more everything.

So it was arranged. Ω, Όπα [Opa]! An engagement party was held in Greece for the happy couple, except there was no couple in Greece because my father was in Ballarat, in the fish and chip shop, having a party of his own. Ω, Όπα [Opa]! My father wrote to my mother and told her not to worry, he said they wouldn't be in Australia long, just long enough to make some money and as soon as they had enough money they would go straight back home—to Greece.

He puts on the black beanie and transforms back into KARAGIOZI, *(Note: this costume change is repeated for all transformations into and out of* KARAGIOZI.)

SCENE SIX: PARASKEVI'S DEPARTURE

KARAGIOZI: Rubbish. You believe that: 'Oh, darlin', as soon as we got enuff money we go back to Greece'. Ahh, you nevah have enuff money! So, Paraskevi engaged to Angelo to come to Australia, is'n she lucky, eh? Takes a coupla months to get the pahpa work togetha, an' when the day come Paraskevi gets ready to leave. All she take with her is a suitcase and photograph of Angelo to help recognise him. I mean, she never met him in her life an' now she's goin' to marry him. So, ten years after Angelo, Paraskevi goes down to the docks with her motha and fatha to say goodbye. No big party for Paraskevi you know, nothin' special, just… goodbye.

> *During the above speech,* KARAGIOZI *moves the suitcase which was the seat in the fish and chip shop to one side and covers it with a black cloth.*

> *He takes his hat off.* PARASKEVI'S MOTHER *bids* PARASKEVI *goodbye.*

MOTHER: Γεια σου παιδί μου, καλό ταξίδι [*Yia sou pethdi mou, kalo taxithi*—Goodbye, my child, have a safe trip].

SCENE SEVEN: PARASKEVI COMES TO AUSTRALIA

PARASKEVI *crosses the stage. When she reaches Australia she pauses to take in her new surroundings, then she gets to work. As she does so, she sings.*

SONG: 'Θάλασσα με πίκρανες' ('Sea, You Have Made Me Bitter')

PARASKEVI: [*sung*]
>
> θάλασσα πως με πίκρανες
> Πως μ' έχεις φαρμακώσει
> Μες την οδό της νιότης μου
> Μ' έχεις βαριά πληγώσει
>
> [Sea, you have made me bitter
> You have poisoned me
> In the track of my youth
> You have buried me]
>
> θάλασσα πως με πίκρανες
> Πως μ' έχεις φαρμακώσει.
>
> [Sea, you have made me bitter
> How you have poisoned me.]

> *She opens her case, takes out an embroidered cloth, and lays it under Angelo's pot plant. Then she opens the large upright box*

on the side of the stage. This is the icon box. Inside we see two religious icons—one of Jesus the other shows the Virgin Mary.

PARASKEVI *lights a candle and kisses an icon. She begins to recite the Lord's Prayer in Greek. She walks to downstage centre and faces the audience. As she walks the Lord's Prayer transforms into* PARASKEVI *practising her English.*

Πάτερ ημών ο εν τοις ουρανοίς
Αγιασθήτω το ονομά σου
Ελθέτω η βασιλεία σου
Γενηθήτω το θελημά σου
Ως εν ουρανώ και επι της γής...

Ee—yes plee, ee—yes plees, yes pleese, yes please, than' you, than' you very martch. Yes please.

She mimes shopping, pointing to what she wants.

Yes please.

She holds up three fingers indicating she wants three items.

Than' you very martch. Ah, mutch!—than' you very mutch.

She points to another item.

Yes, yes please.

She mimes that she wants slices.

Than' you very mutch, yes than' you.

She takes out her money to pay. Not knowing how much is needed, she holds out her hands full of coins to let the shopkeeper take the money.

Than' you. Than' you very mutch.

She hears a new word and tries to work it out.

Bahhy... Bahhyy? Bahyy... Bahyy. Oh, 'bye... 'bye, 'bye-'bye, 'bye-'bye.

SCENE EIGHT: PARASKEVI'S STORIES

ANDREAS: When my mother first arrived she found two forks in my father's kitchen and that was it. My father and his mates used to deep-fry pies in the fish and chip cooker for breakfast.

When she first arrived she stayed with my father's niece and each day she would catch the bus to the fish and chip shop, work with my father, and at night catch a taxi back home. She did this for six months and then they got married. That was her engagement.

PREGNANCY

ANDREAS: When my mother was pregnant with my sister Theodora, she woke up at midnight with cramp and she went downstairs and started ironing to pass the time. She ironed for three hours and then she tidied up the house. She walked up to the hospital, three blocks away, admitted herself, gave birth, and then got out of bed and went to the phone to ring home and wake everyone one up with the good news.

LUNCH AT PRIMARY SCHOOL

ANDREAS: At my primary school there were two other Greek kids—John and Con. And their mother, Throsou, would bring them food at lunchtime. Σούπα, φασολάδα, γεμιστά [*Soupa, fasoulatha, gemista*—Soup, bean stew, stuffed tomatoes]. And she would feed them in the yard at lunchtime in front of everybody. [*He becomes a* YOUNG ANDREAS.] 'Mum… I just want a Vegemite sandwich for lunch.'

A CLEVER WOMAN

MAN 1: Excuse me. Do you know the way to Cameron's Steel Supplies?

ANDREAS: Oh, I don't think Mum would know…

PARASKEVI: Yes, you just go straih' down Sturt Street, turn right at Doveton Street, is right next door to Tarhget.

MAN 1: Thank you. She's a pretty clever woman your mum, son.

A NIGHT-TIME TRIP

ANDREAS: I remember my mother waking me up one night saying, 'Come on, we're going to find your father'. We went downstairs and the house was all dark and we got into the car and Mum drove through the streets of Ballarat late at night. She drove down the bottom of Dana Street hill and she stopped the car and pointed to a house on the corner that had a light on. 'Go and have a look and see if your father is in there.' I just looked at her but she said, 'Go on'. So I went over to the window and reached up and looked inside and there was Dad.

He mimes ANGELO *smoking and playing cards.* ANGELO *despairs as he loses the hand. He reaches into his pockets and takes out all he has and throws it onto the table, nodding to the dealer to start dealing.*

So I went back to the car and told Mum what I had seen and she just sat there for a long time, said nothing. Then she started up the car and we went home.

GREASY WOG

PARASKEVI: [*to Spiro, offstage*] Σπύρο φέρε τσίπς [*Spiro feri chips—*Spiro, bring some chips]… [*To* MAN 2] Salt, on your chips? [*To Spiro*] Πρέπει να ψήσουμε κι άλλα [*Prepi na psisoumai kialla*—We have to cook some more].

MAN 2: Hey, you want to speak your own language, why don't you go back to your own country, you greasy wog!

PARASKEVI *wraps the chips with her head bowed. She is about to hand them over, but changes her mind and throws them in the bin.*

PARASKEVI: You get out from my shop. I know my mother and I know my father. I know who I am. Get out from my shop.

SURPRISE VISIT

ANDREAS: In 1994 my mother went to America, to visit her sister, Agelkoula. Mum hadn't seen Agelkoula since they were young girls together in Greece, more than thirty years. So, Mum decided to pay a surprise visit.

PARASKEVI *knocks on the front door.*

AGELKOULA: Yes please, madam.

PARASKEVI *opens her mouth to speak but can't.*

Madam, what's wrong with you?

PARASKEVI: Could I have a glass of water please?

AGELKOULA: Yes yes. Come inside.

PARASKEVI: Agelkoula, you don't recognise…

AGELKOULA: How you know my name?

PARASKEVI: Aren't I your sister, Paraskevi?

AGELKOULA: Paraskevi? Αχ [Ah]...

ANDREAS: Then they both cried. We all cry whenever Mum tells that story.

LONG DISTANCE

PARASKEVI: [picking up the telephone] Hello. Εμπρός [Embros—Yes]?

She starts shouting down the phone.

Ποιος μιλάει; Γεια σου Λούλα [Pios milae? Yia sou Loula—Who's speaking? Hello Loula].

She calls the family to the phone.

Quick everyone, it's Greece! Τι κάνεις; Είσαι καλά; Εεεε δε σ' ακούω καλά. Δόξα το Θεό [Ti kanies, isay kalah? Eh? Thes akou kalah. Thoxa to theo—How are you, are you well? Hey? I can't hear you. Good, thank God].

Καλά Λούλα, εσείς; Δώσε μου το μικρό [Kala Loula, esis? Thos mou to mikro—Good, Loula, and you? Put the little one on].

She begins to cry.

Γεια σου καμάρι μου τι κάνεις; Όχι καμάρι μου δεν είναι εδύ, δεν είναι εδώ, πήγε στο [Yia sou kamari ti kaneis. Ochi then inay etho. Peegai sto—Hello, my darling, how are you? No, darling, he isn't here, he isn't here he's gone to]...

She struggles to find the words in Greek but can't.

... school today!

SCENE NINE: KARAGIOZI'S ODYSSEY—THE CYCLOPS

KARAGIOZI: Brrr brr, brr brrr.

He takes out the toy phone.

[As O'DYSSEA] Hello, hello, who's speaking? Hello Athena. Yes, darlin', I called before. Oops, sorry darlin', I forgot to put my clothes on.

He puts on the beanie.

Listen, I wan' to speak with your father. I wan' to speak with the big boss, Zeus.

[*To the audience*] Our hero, O'dyssea, is praying to the gods.

O'DYSSEA: Hello Zeus, hello make, how you goin'? Listen here, make—
Yeah, O'dyssea, you know the bloke, who go ta Hell en back—oh, I mean I gotta Helen back. Look, I'm trying to get back home and I'm havin' a bit of trouble—Hello… hello?

KARAGIOZI: O'dyssea our hero is in big, big trouble.

Using his hands he creates an image of the sun rising.

When dawn rose with her ruby red fingers O'dyssea and his men climb aboard their bright beautiful boat and sail across the wine dark sea bound for Ithaca. After many days they land on the shores of a very strange and beautiful island.

O'DYSSEA: Oh, this looks pretty strange and beautiful. Come on, let's have a look and see what we can find. Oh, look, I thin' I found something already, that was quick!

He opens the box and creates an echo effect with his voice.

Hey, looki here, it looks like a, a, cave, cave, cave. It's a cave. Hey yeah, yeah, yeah, look over there, there, there, what's that, that, that? Baaa, baaa, baaa. It's a seep. Hey, boys, let's go inside, oh look, it's not such a small cave.

He drags the box to centre stage.

Oh no, it's a big cave, cave, cave. Oh yeah, yeah, yeah. Oh, look over there, there, there. There's a chair, chair, chair, chair…

He slaps himself.

Stop that! Hey, boys, let's make ourselves at home, have some food.

SAILOR 1: Ah, O'dyssea, I thin' somebody live here and whoever lives here is big, I mean really big. I thin' we sould go. Oh, O'dyssea, I gotta bad feelin'.

The door to the cave closes.

O'dyssea, O'dyssea…

Loud footsteps can be heard from inside the box. The box springs open and the CYCLOPS *is revealed—*KARAGIOZI *with the black beanie pulled down over one eye. The next sequence is performed in mime.*

The CYCLOPS *discovers the intruders, grabs them one by one and eats them. The* CYCLOPS *falls asleep.* O'DYSSEA *climbs up the sleeping* CYCLOPS' *body and blinds him.*

CYCLOPS: Αχ πατέρα ο Οδυσσέας με στράβωσε, αν είμαι πραγματικά ο γιος σου, σπίτι να μη δει ο Οδυσσέας, αλλά αν το έχει γραφτό η μοίρα του, πατρίδα να ξανά δει και να βρει μόνο πόνο εκεί [*Ach patera oh O'dyssea me stravouse, an eemay pragmatika o yios sou spiti na min thei o O'dyseas, alla an to echi graphto I mirra tou patritha na xana thi, na vri mono pono ekei*— Oh Father, Odysseus has blinded me, if I truly am your son, may Odysseus never return home but if it is in his fate he will see his homeland again but there he will only find pain].

The CYCLOPS *jumps back into the box and disappears.*

KARAGIOZI: [*appearing from inside the box*] You understand? You hear what he say? He call to his father Posiedon, he says, 'Father, O'dyssea has blinded me, if I am your son don't let O'dyssea go home, but if he does, make sure he finds only a world of pain at home'. Sounds like trouble to me. But O'dyssea not scared, come on, he's tough, he's Greek. He says, 'Come on, boys, get on the boat, let's go home'.

He closes the box and starts to make the sound of birds whistling.

After another coupla days they land on anotha island. This island belongs to a… very beautiful goddess, her name is Circe and she says…

CIRCE: I know you, you are the very, very famous hero O'dyssea.

O'DYSSEA: [*a little embarrassed*] Awwwhhhh!

CIRCE: And you are a very, very good-looking fellow.

O'DYSSEA: [*flexing his biceps*] Well, I try to after myself.

CIRCE: But you look so tired.

O'DYSSEA: Well, of course I'm tired. I fight at Troy for ten years, poke the eye out of a Cyclops—that's a lot of work, you know.

CIRCE: Why don't you come inside an' have… [*pulling the curtains to her bedroom open*] … a little rest?

O'DYSSEA: Oh, ah well, I ahhh, no I ahhh… [*pointing to his wedding ring*] … well, I ahhh… oh, awright.

The phone rings.

Hello, hello Penelope darlin'. Oh yeah, I miss you too. Well yes, of course I'm coming home, I've just got a bit of a problem, I've got this big... monster I've got to fight. [*Growling at* CIRCE] I fight the monster, I'll be right home. Listen, put Telemache on. Hello, Telemache, how are you? Good, how's you mum, good, how's school good, put your mother back on. What do you mean I've been here for one year?

KARAGIOZI: It's true. Under Circe's spell one whole year has gone by. O'dyssea turns to Circe and says, 'Let me go from your spell, I want to go home', and they climb aboard the boat and sail across the sea.

SCENE TEN: KARAGIOZI'S RAVE

KARAGIOZI: Is'na fantastic story, huh? You see why I love it? I tried to tell Andreas about the otha story—'bout the motha-fatha story—pah! But he doesn' wan' to listen. 'Cause he's the ackta. Nα! [*Na—a gesture and sound combined to indicate someone is an idiot.*] You know he could have been an engineer. Is true. He went to university—Melbourne University—to study engineer, then after one year he come home to his motha and say, 'I don' want to be engineer, I wan' to be ackta'. Nα!

He slaps one hand into the back of the other in the direction of ANDREAS *offstage.*

You know he came to me and he says to me, 'Oh, Karagiozi, I want to tell a big story in the theata 'bout my motha, fatha and when they come from Greece to Afstralia, what life was like'. You know what I sould have said? I sould have said, 'Listen, Andreas, don' waste the time from the people, don' take their money. If people wan' to know I can tell them for free! When your motha, fatha first come from Greece to Afstralia, like me, life was just—boring! That's it, than' you very much, goodnite!' Is truth. Ev'ry single day is jus' the same. Two pices fis', coupla chips, three potato cakes,—ev'ryday—two pices fis', coupla chips, three potato cakes. Eh, if you lucky maybe you get dim sim for something different, but it's the same. You carn do nothin', when you first arrive in a new country you carn go nowhere. You tell me, where you can go? Oh, you can go to the pub. Oh yeah, let's go to the pub.

He becomes a BAR FLY *leaning on the bar at the pub.*

BAR FLY: 'Ello, mate, how'r'you? I've not seen you b'fore. What's yaw name?

KARAGIOZI: My name is Karagiozi, but you can call me Vasili.

BAR FLY: Vasili, Vasili, whadsorda bloody name's that? [*Shouting to others in the pub*] Hey, it's Vasili! [*To* KARAGIOZI] Oh, Vasilly, Vasilly, I'm gonna call you *Frank*!

KARAGIOZI: Where you find Frank from? [*Pause.*] At least if I was in Greece you can go out. Have it good time. If you are very lucky you can go to the—bouzoukia!

He reveals a small bouzouki from the things on the prop table.

You like this? I buy this last time I was in Greece as ενθύμιο [*entheemeo*—keepsake]—to remind me. You want for me to play you somthin'?—Yes, of course.

He prepares to play the bouzouki—stretches his fingers, limbers up. He puts his fingers on the strings about to play but doesn't. Instead he winds it up—it plays 'Never on a Sunday.'

You know this. Oh come on, you mus' know this song. Come on, wake up, Afstralia!

He sings quietly and dances a few steps.

Ah, Greece—Ελλάδα μου [*Ellatha*—My Greece].

He sits on a chair next to the prop table.

But I tell you something—Greece today is not the country I used to know—is not the one I left behind. You undastand?

I tell you somethin'. In Greece today the young girls they smoke on the street, in front of everybody. Oh, not only that, in Greece today the young girls they got boyfriend. Oh, not just one boyfriend, two boyfriend, three boyfriend—the bloody boys got boyfriends too. Oh, the young people in Greece today they shockin'. They don' want to dance the propa Greek dance—you know, ρεμπέτικο, χασάπικο [*rembetiko, chasapiko*—*Greek traditional dances*]—they want to dance disco, American disco. They don't want to drink ρετσίνα [*restina*—*Greek wine*]—you know, beautiful Greek wine, they say, 'Oh no, we want to drink Italia wine'. I say to them, 'Italia wine? You want to drink Italia wine, we fight the bloody Italia in the war, we beat them, but now you want to drink Italia wine!'

I mean, everybody go to Greece today to buy land for holiday home, from Europe everybody go. The Dutch, the Swiss—the Germans! We fight the bloody Germans too—alright we not beat them—but we bloody fight them and now the Germans, they buy Greece from us.

But you know the worse thing about Greece today? The worse thing about Greece today is the bloody Greeks. Come on, tell the truth.

If you go to Greece today, like me—I go back to Greece, I go to the airport I get in the taxi—the driver he say, 'Welcome back to your country, my brother, my friend.' At the same time the meter run faster than Cathy Freeman! Ohh, I go to my village, to my brother, I say to him, 'I come to get the land my father leave for me'—you know, my inheritance. And my brother he says to me, 'Oh no, you took everything with you to Afstralia'. I say, 'I beg you pardon. I beg you pardon, I took one bloody suitcase with me to Afstralia, how much land you can fit in one suitcase?' He says, 'Oh come on, you very rich in Afstralia, you got a lot of money!' I say, 'I got a lot of money! I got a lot of money! I got no bloody hair, make. I work in the factory, in the fis' and chip shop every bloody day, from the bloody week, from the bloody year. You sit in the coffee shop, in the καφενέιο [*kaffeneio*] havin' nice time drinkin' coffee, get up off your bloody bum, go out and do some bloody work and you can have some money too!'

Oh, Greece today is full from bloody *wogs*!

SCENE ELEVEN: THE SLIDE SHOW

KARAGIOZI: [*to the audience*] Hey—you want for me to show you somethin' very funny? A secret between me and all of you. To Andreas.

He puts his finger to his lips indicating silence.

Okay?

He crosses the stage and approaches an audience member with the remote control lead of a slide projector.

You can help me? Is very easy, you don have to worry. You see the white button, when I say yes, you press—tsak—just like that, just quick. When I say yes, you press. Press when I say yes, press yes, yes press—you got it? You very clever, very clever. Wait, wait, wait you must be Greek. You not Greek. You sure? I like you anyway.

Alternative—if the audience member responds yes: 'Really! I knew it. Which part of Greece you from? Ah well, nobody's perfect.'

[*To the lighting operator*] Okay, turn off the light.

He opens the lid of the prop box to form a projector screen onto which the images of a slide show are projected.

[*To the audience member*] Okay, you ready, steady, and *yes!*

Slide 1: ANDREAS *as a baby.*

Hey, look at this. Who's this? It's Andreas. *Yes.*

Slide 2: ANGELO *on a boat.*

Oh, look at it. This is Angelo, here, Andreas' father, on the boat come from Greece to Afstralia. 1950, the boat was the *San Giorgio. Yes.*

Slide 3: A portrait of PARASKEVI.

It's Paraskevi. Paraskevi, the mother from Andreas, you know. This is when she is come from Greece to Afstralia, twenty years old. You know, she's not speak one word from English. In Greek we say λούλούδι [*loulouthe*—beautiful flower]. *Yes.*

Slide 4: A bridal car.

Ohh, the wedding! Lookadi, Angelo, Paraskevi, horseshoe, eh? *Yes.*

Slide 5: The fish'n'chip shop.

Oh, fis' and chips. Look, we got Angelo, we got Paraskevi, we got… chips. Ah look, very important. This is propa fis' and chips, with the newspapah. *Yes.*

Slide 6: Family photo of two kids.

Oh, coupla kids. You know the Greeks don' waste any time—tsak tsak. This is Thea and this baby Spiro. *Yes.*

Slide 7: Family photo of four kids.

Four kids even fasta work. This is Thea, Spiro, new baby Theodora. Who's this one? It's Andreas. *Yes.*

Slide 8: Angelo at a party.

Hey, that's Angelo and it looks like his havin' a party! Yeah, havin' a party in a milk bar. Havin' a party in a milk bar—where you can go. *Yes.*

Above: Angelo Litras (back row, fourth from the left) aboard the San Giorgio *bound for Australia 1950 with the contingent of Greek travellers aboard the boat. Below: Angelo and Paraskevi Litras in their Ballarat fish and chip shop, Angelo's Fish and Chips, 721 Sturt Street, Ballarat, circa 1970.*

Slide 9: A mule.

This is Greece. This is 1976 when Andreas and Theodora go to Greece for three months with their mother. [*He points to Andreas' clothes.*] How's this for a fashion statement? Now this is very importan', pleas' listen careful. [*He points to the mule.*] In Greek we call this one Μουλάρι [*Moulari—Mule*]. Remember this word, because if someone in Greek say to you you are Μουλάρι, this is what you are. *Yes.*

Slide 10: Fish and chip wedding.

It's a wedding, oh here comes the bride. It's a wedding in a fis' and chip shop! This is Loula, the sister from Paraskevi, she comes from Greece to Afstralia when she was sixteen years old. She stay for coupla years with Angelo and Paraskevi in the fis' and chip shop then after that she get married to Yanni and then they open up their own fis' and chips. Is'na romantic? *Yes.*

Slide 11: Another wedding.

Oh Laykia, you know from Melton. Laykia is the nephew from Angelo, he's come from Greece to Afstralia, stay with Angelo an' Paraskevi and after coupla years he gets married to Vassou and they went to Melton and then they open up a fruit shop. Oh no, no it was'na', it was a fis' and chips. *Yes.*

Slide 12: Yet another wedding.

Oh, Varvara. Varvara is the niece from Paraskevi, she's come from Greece to Afstralia, stay with Angelo, Paraskevi, then after that she gets married to George, they go to Ferntree Gully and open up, now what was it… it was a… Yeah, you right—fis' and chips. You know fis' and chips is very important to this country. To tell the truth this whole country is built on fis' and chips. An' all it takes is one stupik politician up in Queensland to open her mouth and she give fis' and chips a bad reputation. *Yes.*

Slide 13: A funeral.

Yes.

Slide 14: Another funeral photo.

He closes the box and collects the remote.

SCENE TWELVE: ANGELO'S DEATH

ANDREAS: [*standing in the projector light*] In 1976 my father had a stroke. I was nine. My last memory of him is him smiling through the plastic tubes coming out of his nose. At six o'clock in the morning my mother rang the hospital...

PARASKEVI: [*on the phone*] Hello. Mrs Litras speakin', I just wan' to check everything alright, yes, yes, yes than' you very much, alright, 'bye-'bye.

ANDREAS: One hour later the phone rang.

PARASKEVI: [*on the phone again*] Hello. Mrs Litras speaking, yes, yes, yes, than' you very much, alright, 'bye-'bye.

> *She opens her mouth as if to scream. Music plays: 'Κατω απ το γέρο πλάτανο' [Kut up toh yehro plahtahno— 'Under the Old Plane Tree']. She raises her hands pleading to the gods.*

> *She transforms into* ANDREAS *who walks forward to the suitcase. He lifts the black cloth and looks underneath at the case—it is a coffin. He lifts the case and carries it across the stage. He places it on the floor, removes the cloth and crosses back to the prop table.*

> *As he does so, a light comes up on the suitcase—it becomes a headstone. The music fades. He picks up flowers and a bucket of water and becomes* PARASKEVI *once more.*

Dora, Andrew, come on kids, in the car. Ελα [*Elah*—Come on], quick.

> *She crosses to the headstone. As she approaches she starts to sing. She kneels, washes Angelo's grave, and places the flowers on the grave, then crosses to the icon box. She returns with an incense burner, lights the incense, and places the burner on the headstone. She returns to the icon box, takes the candle and exits behind the icon box. The voice changes to* KARAGIOZI—*he enters with a candle, singing the same song.*

SONG: 'Η Ξενιτια' ('The Foreign Lands')

> Ο θάνατός και η ξενιτιά,
> η πίκρα και η αγάπη

τα τέσσερα ζυγίστηκαν
σ' ένα χρυσό καδάρι

[Death, the foreign lands,
Bitterness and love
The four were weighed
On scales of gold]

Το πιο βαρύ η ξενιτιά
Το πιο βαρύ απ' ολα

[The heaviest? the foreign lands
The heaviest of all]

Ο ξένος εις στην ξενιτιά
Πρέπει να φοράει μαύρα
Για να ταιριάζει η φορεσιά
Με της καρδιάς τη λάμπα.

[A stranger in the foreign lands
Has to wear black
To match his attire
To his heart's burning flame.]

SCENE THIRTEEN: THE UNDERWORLD

Through the following speech KARAGIOZI *sets the stage up for the Underworld. He lays the prop box on its side, forming a table.*

KARAGIOZI: O'dyssea! You have to go to the Underworld. Αντε μωρέ μη μου το λες [*Ach mi mou to les*—Oh, don't tell me]. You must journey to the Land of the Dead. Oh no! Yes! You must find Tiresias, the blind seer. Sail in your ship to the end of the world. When you arrive leave all your men on the ship, take with you only one seep [*sheep*].

He places the make-up case on the table and he becomes a sheep.

Baaa. Baaa. Baaa.

He mimes the sheep getting its throat cut.

Dig a trench, cut the throat of the seep and fill the trench with the blood an' you will summon the spirits of the dead to you.

O'dyssea arrives at the door to the Underworld. O'dyssea opens the doors to the Underworld.

A floor light comes on as he opens the case and peers inside—it is the Underworld.

'Hello, anybordy home? Uhh, I'm lookin' for Mr Tiresias. Hello Mr Tiresias, looking for Mr Tiresias, you know the blind see-ah. I mean, I don' know how he can see if his blind. Anyhow, looking for Mr Tiresias, Mr Tiresias. Wait. Mr Tiresias…

KARAGIOZI *disappears into the case and emerges with a white painted face.*

TIRESIAS: Oh, O'dyssea, Man of Pain, stand back! Let me drink the blood and I will tell you all of the truth.

He disappears and emerges with a bloody mouth.

Ahh, O'dyssea, a swift journey home is what you desire, but you must control your desire, do not let your men touch the cattle of the sun god Illios, ahhhhh!

O'DYSSEA: Tiresias, come back, I got to ask you… Oh no… You carn be dead, I left you alive in Ithaca, Mother. Μάνα [*Mana*—Mother], you carn be dead… You carn be dead…

KARAGIOZI *emerges as* O'DYSSEA'S MOTHER *with a mop head for hair.*

MOTHER: Yes, my son, I am dead. I died waiting for you to come home' but Penelope, she's alive and waiting for you to go home. But there are all these suitors trying to woo her and steal you kingdom. You must hurry and return home. Arrghh, O'dyssea, O'dysseaaaaa…

She cries. As she disappears, the cry changes as the voice becomes deeper. KARAGIOZI *emerges with a crown as* CAPTAIN AGAMEMNON.

AGAMEMNON: Aarrghhh. Yeeees, O'dyssea, I too am dead. My wife Clytamenestra killed me when I got home from Troy, but that's another Greek story. Be careful, O'dyssea, be careful when you go home, Penelope might try to kill you too!

O'DYSSEA'S MOTHER *reappears.*

MOTHER: No, O'dyssea, Penelope love you, she never goin' to hurt you.

AGAMEMNON: Yes, I thought my wife love me too but look what she did to me.

MOTHER: That's because you stupik.

AGAMEMNON: I'm not stupik, I'm a king.

MOTHER: Listen to me, O'dyssea.

AGAMEMNON: No, O'dyssea, to me.

MOTHER: O'dyssea, O'dyssea...

AGAMEMNON: O'dyssea, O'dyssea...

> KARAGIOZI *slams the suitcase shut on the Underworld and they disappear.*

KARAGIOZI: Very scary, wasn' ah? O'dyssea goes back to the ship. He says nothing of what he has seen, he just says, 'Come on, boys, get on the boat. Let's go home.'

> KARAGIOZI *takes the candle back to the icon box and then puts the Underworld suitcase away. He takes off the beanie and becomes* ANDREAS. ANDREAS *picks up the washbasin, towel and soap, goes centre stage and begins washing his face.*

SCENE FOURTEEN: FACEWASHING

ANDREAS: After my father died everything in our lives changed. My brother became my father and my sister became my mother. My mother just worked in the shop. Every day except for Christmas, that's why Christmas Day was special for us because it was the only day of the year that the shop was shut. The only day we could sit down together as a family and eat a meal in peace.

Everybody helped out in the shop. I made the chips out the back till I was tall enough to reach the counter when I was ten.

I remember locking up the record player for a year, as part of πένθος² [*penthos*]—the official Greek mourning period. My mother thought about locking up the television too but she decided that having four small kids, a business to run, and no television wasn't such a good idea.

Because my mother was a widow and had four small kids and a business to run, we didn't go out to parties or celebrations and because

---

² Traditionally no songs are sung or music played for a year after the death of a family member. The women of the family wear black as a sign of their mourning.

my mother was a widow and had four small kids and a business to run, people stopped coming around. So gradually we lost contact.

At primary school it was a novelty having a fish and chip shop, at high school it just made me a 'wog'. Not all the time, just once or twice, but that was enough. So I stopped speaking Greek and I stopped wanting to have anything to do with the Greeks. I didn't want to be Greek.

He returns the washbasin to the props table.

SCENE FIFTEEN: THE JOURNEY BACK TO GREECE

ANDREAS: Then when I first moved to Melbourne I went looking for a job. I walked into a Greek restaurant and asked to speak to the manager. I said, 'I'm looking for a job and I don't know if it helps but I'm actually Greek'. The manager just looked at me and said, 'You're Greek?' I said, 'Yeah'. 'You're Greek? Great, 'cause I'm not!' He said, 'I keep on trying to convince people that I'm Greek but they never believe me they say, "Oh, Malcom—you're not Greek".' But Malcom said to me, 'If you work here and you're Greek and you don't look it, well then they might believe that I'm Greek, even though I'm not'. So I got the job.

And Malcom would go around to the tables saying, 'I am Greek! Look at Andrew, he's Greek, he doesn't look it.' And the customers would speak to me in Greek and I could barely string a sentence together and I felt ashamed.

A year later I went to Greece for my cousin's wedding. I remember looking out the plane window and all I could see was blue—clear and bright.

There was a taxi driver waiting for me at the airport, a man called Kosta. In Kosta's taxi I had my first conversation in Greek. Kosta asked me, 'Οδηγάς' [*Othigas*]? Which means 'Do you drive?' I know that now but then I just looked back and said, 'Wha'?' He pointed to the steering wheel and the car and finally I got it. I said, 'Oh ναι, yes, yes, δραιβέρνο και έχω κάρο'[3] [*drive-erno kai echxo car-o*—I drive and I have a car]. The only problem is, 'drive-erno'

---

[3] This sentence would not make sense to a Greek-speaking person for two reasons. Firstly the word 'drive-erno' doesn't exist and secondly, the word 'car-o' actually means a horse-drawn cart. 'Car' is αυτοκήνιτο [*aftokinito*]—automobile.

doesn't actually exist in Greek. It's one of those Greek-Australian words that only exists here. It's what we call Gringlish. Gringlish is basically English with a Greek sound stuck on the end. So no-one understood a thing 'cause all I knew were Gringlish words like fridge-ah, and doct-ah, or better still there's roof-ee and floor-ee.

Finally the taxi pulled up and at the end of the driveway there were three chairs—my aunt, uncle and cousin were sitting in the chairs, they'd been sitting there all afternoon in the sun waiting because they knew someone was coming from Australia, they didn't know who but they knew someone was coming. Well, as soon as they saw the taxi pull up they just got up and started racing towards me and my auntie is a very big woman. I wasn't even out of the taxi door when I was just smothered.

That night I was the guest of honour at my cousin's wedding and the same aunt came up to me with a big smile and said, 'You're the special guest and I've saved this for you'.

She plonked down a platter in front of me and I looked down and there was a roast sheep's head. My cousin sitting next to me jabs me in the ribs and says, 'Ah, you lucky bugger, you got the best bit. Here I'll show you what to do.' He reached over, grabbed the top to the skull and ripped it off and I looked down and I could see the brains inside. And my cousin was just smiling at me. So I picked up a fork and dug it in. It was thick and pastey. I gave it to my cousin to finish.

Everywhere I went in Greece I was retracing my footsteps—the footsteps of an eight-year-old. Rediscovering things from my first childhood visit to Greece that I didn't even know I still remembered. Like the taste of fresh goats' milk, still warm, or the sound of the bells on the sheep that were grazing way up on the mountain. And I would go looking for the buildings that I was sure that I could find—the ones that stood out huge in my memory. I would arrive somewhere and think, this is it, this is the place, but I would be frustrated because nothing seemed right. Then I would take my time, look around some more and realise that I was there, that I had found what I was looking for, it's just that the scale was all wrong.

I went to my father's village and this old lady, tiny, all dressed in black, stopped me in the street. 'Πιανού είσαι εσύ?' [*'Pianou eisai esi?* '] Whose son are you? And I looked down into her face and I said, 'Είμαι το παιδί του Ευάγγελου—Γιάννης' [*'Eimai to pedhi tou Evangelo—Yianni'*]. 'I'm Angelo's son'. And she took my hand and looked up into my face and said, 'Αχ που είναι ο πατέρας τώρα;' [*'Ach pou einai o pateras tora'*], 'Where is your father now?'

And I went to my father's house, and as I came around the bend in the road I could see my uncle, my father's brother, sitting on the balcony, and just for a moment my heart stopped. I thought I saw a ghost.

After six months in Greece I came back to Australia. Everyone in Greece called me Τον Αυστραλό [*Ton Afstralo*]—the Australian—so I knew where to go. When I got back one of the first things I did was change my name. Because even though I had been baptised Andreas after my παππούλη [*papouli*]—my grandfather—I had been called Andrew all my life. And I never ever liked Andrew. So I gave myself the gift of my own name.

SCENE SIXTEEN: THE FINAL JOURNEY HOME

KARAGIOZI: O'dyssea begins the final journey home. They sail away from the Underworld. They sail past the Sirens singing their song, luring them to their death. O'dyssea says, 'Don't listen to the song of the Sirens'. [*He blocks his ears.*] 'I'm not listening, I'm not listening', and the boat goes safely past.

They sail past the Scylla, high in the rocks with her six heads, she snatches down and eats six men. Charybdis opens up and swallows the ocean floor, but the boat goes past. Then they see the island of Illios, with the fat, sleek cattle grazing. O'dyssea says, 'Boys, remember what Tiresias said, don' touch the sacred cattle, don' touch the sacred…'

'Oh no, we not goin' to touch them, we goin' to eat them.' And they do. Illios tells Zeus who sends down a thunderbolt and everyone is dead except O'dyssea. Then finally he arrives on… another island. This island belongs to… another beautiful goddess. Her name is Calypso.

O'DYSSEA: 'Oh, hello, Calypso. I'm very tired, do you mind if I stay, just for a couple of days?'

The phone rings. O'DYSSEA *looks around to find the source of the sound. Calypso tells him that it is his phone. He answers it.*

Hello? Who? Oh, I don't know. Yeah, alright, I'll check, just a moment, hold on. [*Searching around*] Is a Penelope here? Is a Penelope here? Is a… [*Realising finally*] Oh, is a Penelope here! Hello, darlin', I'm sorry, I not recognise your voice. What do you mean I been here for seven years!'

KARAGIOZI: It's true. Seven years have gone by. He turns to Calypso and says, 'Calypso, please let me go from your spell'. And finally he arrive in Ithaca! He sees his son Telemechos, remember the baby, now his a grown man, twenty years old. And he sees all the blokes who try to marry his wife and—tsak, tsak, tsak—he kill the bloody lot. And then he sees, 'Penelope! Penelope, it's me, it's your husband, O'dyssea. I'm home'. And Penelope says, 'Wait a minute, buster, how I know you're my husband, it's been twenty years, that's a long time and people change. You have to prove you are my husband.'

'Prove it? I can prove it. No problem. You Penelope, have a birth-mark, a little olive just down there, right behind the knee.' And Penelope says, 'Aw come on, all the boys know that one'.

'Awright, I can prove it propa. In you bedroom there was an olive tree—an ελιά [*elia*]. I know because I cut that tree down and from the stump I make the bed. No-one can move the bed from the bedroom because the roots—οι ρίζες [*ee rizes*]—are still deep into the ground—βαθιά' [*vathia*—deep].'

Penelope she hear this she start to cry, she say, 'Ναι είσαι πραγματικά ο άνδρας μου' [*'Isay pragmatika o andras mou'*—'You are, in truth, my husband']. Only my husband and I know that secret. After twenty years you are O'dyssea and you are home.'

Now that's what I call a proper Greek story.

> KARAGIOZI *removes his beanie. Through the next speech,* ANDREAS *takes the incense off the headstone and returns it to the icon box. He then picks up the suitcase.*

ANDREAS: I asked my mother why she never went back to Greece to live. She told me that she had spent more years of her life living in Australia than she ever had in Greece and that as a woman she was freer living here than she ever would have been in Greece. But also

she said that all her children were born here and that her husband
was buried here in this soil, and that makes this our home.

*He starts to sing. As he does so, he turns to walk upstage. The
suitcase leaves a trail of soil behind it. When he reaches the centre
upstage box* ANDREAS *turns to face the audience. The lights slowly
fade as the song continues.*

SONG: 'Μια χούφτα χώμα ελληνικό' ('A Handful of Greek Earth')
reprise

Μια χούφτα χώμα Ελληνικό
Για φυλαχτό θα πάρω
Τώρα που πάω στην Ξενιτιά
Να μη φοβάμαι κανένα Χάρο

[A handful of Greek earth
As a keepsake I'll take
Now that I'm going to the foreign lands
So that I will fear no ill fate]

Δεν θα ξεχάσω το χωριό
Όσο καιρό θα αργήσω
Στο σπίτι μου το πατρικό
Γρήγορα θα γυρίσω

[I will not forget my village
No matter how long I am gone
To my father's house
I'll quickly return]

Μια χούφτα χώμα ελληνικό
Στον κόρφο μου θα κρίψο
Να το 'χώ για παρηγορία
Οσο καιρό θα αργήσω

[A handful of Greek earth
I'll hide in my breast
To have for my solace
For as long as I am delayed.]

On the last note of the song the stage lights fade to black.

THE END

www.currency.com.au

Visit Currency Press' website now to:

- Buy your books online
- Browse through our full list of titles, from plays to screenplays, books on theatre, film and music, and more
- Choose a play for your school or amateur performance group by cast size and gender
- Obtain information about performance rights
- Find out about theatre productions and other performing arts news across Australia
- For students, read our study guides
- For teachers, access syllabus and other relevant information
- Sign up for our email newsletter

The performing arts publisher

www.ingramcontent.com/pod-product-compliance
Lightning Source LLC
Chambersburg PA
CBHW041935090426
42744CB00017B/2064